The Art of Surrender: Making the Case for a Christ-Centered Life

AUTHOR: MICHAEL BODDIE II

EDITOR: RENEE LEE

CONTENTS

CHAPTER 1

WORTH

You have more endurance than you realize. In addition, your multitasking skills are unmatched. Whether we have met before or not, I can stand upon those statements without having any doubt that they are true because right now, you are doing the impossible. At this very moment, as you are relaxing in your reclining chair at home, laying in a hammock, silently reading at a library, or reading in some other circumstance, you are also running. Every person that has ever existed or ever will exist, including myself, has, is, or will spend the entirety of their existence running.

At this point, you probably have deduced that I am not talking about the literal physical act of running. I am talking about the spiritual pursuit of ultimate fulfillment. Some people chase after fame and fortune. Others, called hedonists, seek pleasure above all else. Then there are some, who the apostle Paul, in 2 Timothy 3:5 NASB, says are "holding to a form of [b]godliness although they have denied its power…" In other words, they are religious but do not have Jesus in their hearts. Finally, praise God, there is a group who through the power of The Holy Spirit is seeking to get as close to God as possible. Yet, the common denominator is that everyone is seeking something.

It is an immutable fact that God created everyone with the need for more than our present reality. Why? It is like how a newborn baby inherently needs to be connected to the love, and dependent on the protection, of their parents. It is more about survival than luxury. The truth is that in the grand scheme of things, we are more helpless than a newborn baby. We cannot save ourselves. We cannot do anything good without the help of God.

No matter what you are pursuing, it is hard to run forever. There are times when we all want to quit and reconsider why we are running in the first place. The first question to ask is if what you are chasing is worth your exhaustion. The unchangeable fact is that God created us to be conduits. In other words, we are never in ultimate control. We are either going to surrender to God or the enemy. Which is worth your surrender?

According to the Bible, our Creator is One who has never had a selfish thought. One of my favorite Scriptural passages, Romans 5:6-11, says, "[6] For while we were still helpless, at *the* right time Christ died for the ungodly. [7] For one will hardly die for a righteous person; [d]though perhaps for the good person someone would even dare to die. [8] But God demonstrates His own love toward us, in that while we were still sinners, Christ died for us. [9] Much more then, having now been justified [c]by His blood, we shall be saved from the wrath *of God* through Him. [10] For if while we were enemies we were reconciled to God through the death of His Son, much more, having been reconciled, we shall be saved [f]by His life. [11] And not only *this*, but [g]we also celebrate in God through our Lord Jesus Christ, through whom we have now received the reconciliation."

Another important scripture is John 10:7-10 because it helps us to understand the actual role and character of Jesus Christ. These verses say "[7] So Jesus said to them again, "Truly, truly I say to you, I am the door of the sheep. [8] All those who came before Me are thieves and robbers, but the sheep did not listen to them. [9] I am the door; if anyone enters through Me, he will be saved, and will go in and out and find pasture. [10] The thief comes only to steal and kill and destroy; I came so that they would have life, and [h]have *it* abundantly." The great thing about Jesus, is that following Him leads to eternal rest. However, following Satan leads to eternal damnation. What would it look like if we made Jesus Our Primary Pursuit? What if we ran to God instead of away from Him? The blessing is that no matter how far we have run from God, He has not run from us. In other words, He thinks that you are worth more than anything in the universe. Choose Jesus. Choose life.

Personal Application:

How does understanding God's love for you influence your view of Him?

_____

_____

_____

_____

_____

_____

_____

_____

What can you do today to make sure that Jesus is number one in your life?

_____

_____

_____

_____

_____

_____

_____

_____

_____

CHAPTER 2

WHO IS GOD?

Your understanding of God will ultimately impact every area of your life. There are so many people who feel hopeless because they do not understand the real character and identity of Jesus Christ. I would also like to suggest that it is not good enough to know of God. Instead, He wants a personal relationship with every one of us. I believe that if people understood the genuine character and identity of Jesus Christ, they would not run from Him. Allow me to explain.

Jesus is the epitome of everything good wrapped into one person. In other words, whatever good thing you lack can be found in Jesus. Is it your health? Jesus can heal you! Is it your finances? Jesus can provide for you! Is it your anxiety? Jesus can calm you! Is it your marriage? Jesus can mend it for you! But most importantly, if it is your eternal salvation, Jesus can save you!

In 1 John 4:8, the Bible says, "[8] The one who does not love does not know God, because God is love." The Bible is full of many other verses that advocate for the selfless and benevolent heart of God. What would it look like if we believed that God is for us?

5

What would it look like if we believed that God only wants what is best for us? What would it look like if we understood that there is never a reason to fear because God, The Champion of The Universe, has a soft spot in His heart for every human ever created? Well, the incredible reality is that all of this is true!

God wants us to have abundant life, not only in heaven but also starting right now! God is the answer to all of life's problems. Therefore, if we trust and obey Him, we will gain access to the best life possible. God is on our side! Although I grew up in church for most of my life, I did not understand the implications of God's love. However, He eventually helped me to see that I do not have to do good works for Him to love or save me. God loves us despite us! Thus, we can have the greatest hope in the world.

Perhaps, the following illustration will make it more transparent. The President of the United States of America holds the highest position in the free world. The character of this leader has a major impact on every citizen for good or bad. The hope for a high quality of life is contingent on the ability of this leader to be compassionate and ethical. Therefore, it is paramount that the leader of the free world be someone who cares for people.

For example, President Trump's character has caused fear and anxiety for some people because they did not trust that he had their best interest at heart. However, I am so glad that we have a God who is higher than any earthly ruler. Our God loves us more than He loves Himself. He went through the agony of a Roman crucifixion for our salvation! He was demonstrating that He would rather lose His own life than have even one of us lose ours.

God is love. He is faithful. He is patient. He is kind. He is selfless. He is omnipotent, which means all-powerful. He is omniscient, which means all-knowing. He is omnipresent, which means He is everywhere at the same time. He is everything that we need. He is our ultimate source of hope.

Personal Application:

Who or what are you allowing to shape your view of God? Is this view Biblically accurate?

_____

_____

_____

_____

_____

_____

_____

_____

_____

How can your life be enhanced by understanding that God's character is love?

_____

_____

_____

_____

_____

_____

_____

_____

_____

CHAPTER 3

BAD THEOLOGY

Have you ever gone through a dark time in your life, and it seemed like it would never end? Most, if not all, people have. I am not exempt from this group. I have gone through various ups and downs in my life. However, the absolute most challenging time started for me around the end of my sophomore year of college. Little did I know at the time that God would use that season to help grow my faith in, and dependence on, Him.

For most of my life, I was perfectly healthy. I had no significant personal or medical disruptions. However, near the end of my sophomore year of college, I started to have a hard time thinking clearly. It was like my faulty understanding of God and the Bible had run its course, and life no longer made sense. For about four years, my thinking was cloudy because I had no peace. I was working so hard to appease God, that I began to feel like He was a tyrant, and I began to hate Him.

I used to feel that I needed to punish myself for the bad

decisions I had made. However, God helped me to see that it was not necessary. By God's grace I now, as a chaplain resident, can help patients and others realize that God does not want us to harm ourselves to please Him. As I often say, God is more concerned about our spiritual growth than our mistakes. In other words, God's reflex is not punishment. It is redemption.

One of the primary reasons that I had a hard time thinking clearly during that dark period in my life was that I did not understand God's real character and identity. I had believed in false theology, which convinced me that it was not possible to know that salvation was sure until Jesus returns. Heaven was a prize to be won. My Christian denomination's doctrines and religious practices made me feel that we were superior to other Christian denominations. I believed that Jesus died on the cross, but there was still work for me to do if I wanted to spend eternity with Him. I did not love God. I just did not want to go to hell.

My life was ruined by bad theology, and sadly this false teaching is also destroying the lives of many others. However, it is my prayer that people will be set free by the following declarations! God loves you! You may be thinking, "How can God love me? I have done too many bad things in my life." My friends, God's love for us is not contingent upon what we do or do not do. God loves us because He created us. Therefore, we are loved by God, even before we exist on this earth. It does not matter what you have done, how many times you did it, or your current circumstance. There is hope because God unconditionally loves you.

You may not believe me, and you should not accept anything people say without checking the facts. So, let us see what the Bible says about the nature of God's love for humanity. Romans 8:31-39 says, "[31] What then shall we say to these things? If God *is* for us, who *is* against us? [32] He who did not spare His own Son, but delivered Him over for us all, how will He not also with Him freely give us all things? [33] Who will bring charges against God's elect? God is the one who justifies; [34] who is the one who condemns? Christ Jesus is He who died, but rather, was [s]raised, who is at the right hand of God, who also intercedes for us. [35] Who will separate us from the love of [t]Christ? *Will* tribulation, or trouble, or persecution, or famine, or nakedness, or danger, or sword? [36] Just as it is written:
"For Your sake, we are killed all day long;
We were regarded as sheep to be slaughtered."
[37] But in all these things we overwhelmingly conquer through Him who loved us. [38] For I am convinced that neither death, nor life, nor angels, nor principalities, nor things present, nor things to come, nor powers, [39] nor height, nor depth, nor any other created thing will be able to separate us from the love of God that is in Christ Jesus our Lord."

We need to be like the Bereans spoken about in the book of Acts. They were declared to have a more noble character because after hearing the Word of God preached, they went back to the Scriptures to study for themselves to determine if what they heard was true. I am not saying that it is never beneficial to receive truth through other ministers or people in general. However, it is easy to believe a falsehood. The greatest crisis in the world is people misunderstanding the heart of God. Perhaps, the hope we desperately seek is not necessitated by God changing; maybe instead, it is our perspective of Him that needs to change.

Personal Application:

How has bad theology impacted your life?

_____

_____

_____

_____

_____

_____

_____

_____

_____

What would it look like if you studied the Bible to get a more accurate picture of God's true character?

_____

_____

_____

_____

_____

_____

_____

_____

_____

_____

CHAPTER 4

TRUE SURRENDER

What does it look like to surrender to Jesus? Is it merely modifying our behavior, or is there more to it? The unfortunate truth is that many people believe that they are submitting to God by changing their actions. However, the Bible clearly states that God does not just want us to change what we do. The true surrender that God wants us to have is when we allow Him to change who we are.

Obedience begins in the heart. There are at least two Biblical passages that make this explicitly clear. In Proverbs 23:6-8, it says

"[6] Do not eat the bread of [d]a selfish person;

Or desire his delicacies;

[7] For as he [e]thinks within himself, so he is.

He says to you, "Eat and drink!"

But his heart is not with you.

[8] You will vomit up [f]the morsel you have eaten

And waste your [g]compliments."

In other words, a person's actions do not always reveal who they are.

God does not want people just to follow Him in action. He wants a genuine relationship with all of us. Thus, He wants us to obey Him because we love Him and not for any other reason.

Another Biblical passage that makes this clear is 1 Samuel 16:6-7. In this situation, God had sent Samuel the prophet to anoint one of the sons of a man named Jesse to be the next king of Israel. The verses say, "[6] When they entered, he looked at Eliab and thought, "Surely the Lord's anointed is *standing* before Him." [7] But the Lord said to Samuel, "Do not look at his appearance or at the height of his stature, because I have rejected him; for [d]God does not *see* as man sees, since man looks at [e]the outward appearance, but the Lord looks at the heart."

Anybody can do the right action. However, God wants us to follow Him in motive and action. The Bible makes it abundantly clear that we are not able to do this on our own. According to Philippians 2, humans are so imperfect that we cannot even want to do what is right unless God intervenes and helps us do it. The road to surrender is not working from the outside to the inside. It is birthed from the inside out.

Back in 2016, I attended a youth rally. One of the featured speakers said something that changed my Christian experience forever. He essentially said that if Christianity is hard for us, then we are not doing it correctly. In other words, following God can be difficult. However, it should not feel like a burden. Growing in our relationship with Jesus Christ should be a labor of love.

Just think about it, would you want to be in a relationship

with someone who is only there out of obligation? God does not want that either. His petition to every one of us today is to let Him into our hearts. It can be hard to be obedient. Full submission to God can be difficult. However, it is always worth it. As a result of true surrender, one thing will become unmistakably evident: There is no one or nothing better than Jesus Christ. When we surrender to Him, we gain so much. He will give us joy, peace, hope, love, and most importantly, eternal life in which there will be no more separation between Him and us. The question is not, can we afford to surrender to God? Instead, the question is, how can we afford not to? He wants to bless and ultimately save each one of us. We can trust God.

Personal Application:

What can you do to help your heart be one that loves God?

_____

_____

_____

_____

_____

_____

_____

_____

_____

How can you use the knowledge learned in this chapter to help others?

_____

_____

_____

_____

_____

_____

_____

_____

_____

_____

_____

CHAPTER 5

THE LIFEGUARD

Jesus is the answer to all of life's problems. I believe that this fact has been made clear. However, there is a difference between knowing the solution and receiving Him. I am convinced that most people's biggest struggle, in terms of their spiritual lives, is not knowing that they need God. The trouble comes in trusting and obeying Him.

When I was doing my undergraduate studies, I researched God's existence for one of my classes. As part of the research, I interviewed different people about whether they believe that God is real and their rationale for their conclusion. One interview, in particular, stands out in my memory. The interviewee was a fellow student who claimed to be an atheist. I asked him why he believed that God was not real. He essentially told me that he does not find it hard to believe that a higher power exists. However, his issue was having to serve that higher power. In other words, he did not like the idea of being inferior to anyone.

It is the most significant quandary in existence. Why do we as humans resist our Creator? He only wants good for us. Yet, we will run to so many other sources to try to find ultimate fulfillment before we will even think test God. He desires to help us. However, we feel that we know better than Him. Therefore, we have this constant struggle of battling to trust and obey Him or put our allegiance elsewhere.

It is much like the parent-child dynamic. Most children go through a phase, or more extended period, of rebellion and resistance to their parents. Yet, the irony is that, if we have good parents, they are our most prominent advocates in this world. They are willing to sacrifice their desires to help our dreams come true. However, we will run from them and trust our immature and foolish friends instead. The more we resist, the harder our lives become.

This concept can also be illustrated through the role of a lifeguard. I am not an avid swimmer. However, I know enough to know that I do not want to swim in a deep pool unless a qualified lifeguard is present. The lifeguard's responsibility is to save those in distress in a particular area of the pool or beach. Interestingly, no matter how skilled and efficient the lifeguard is at their job, it becomes difficult, if not impossible, to rescue a drowning person who is trying to save themselves. In other words, the more the drowning person flounders around, instead of surrendering themselves to the life-saving efforts of the lifeguard, the more they are counter-productive. To be saved, they need to rest and depend on the lifeguard.

In Isaiah 64:6, it says "…For all of us have become like one who is unclean,
And all our righteous deeds are like a filthy garment;". In other words, we cannot save ourselves. We are so flawed that even our attempts to do good are wrong because of our corrupt hearts. On the other hand, God is perfect. He is the very essence of unconditional love. We need Him. So, the next time that we feel Him tugging at our hearts to give Him our lives, will, and allegiance, let us not focus on the price. Instead, we need to pray for God to help us focus on the prize.

It can be easy to become discouraged in the process of our spiritual growth. Sometimes we may feel God petitioning us to stop looking at pornography or return a faithful tithe and offering. At other times, we may struggle to be honest in a situation where the truth will not make us appear in a flattering light. However, it will become easier to surrender to God when we do not focus on what we must give up for Him. Instead, by the power of The Holy Spirit, focus on what Jesus has given up for us. He left the honor, glory, majesty, and splendor of heaven to die on a wooden rugged cross in our place. In response, He is inviting us to be faithful to Him. Being faithful to Christ does not mean that we will be flawless. Yet, it will become apparent that the greatest blessings can only be found through Jesus Christ.

Personal Application:

Are you resisting God in any area of your life?

_____

_____

_____

_____

_____

_____

_____

_____

_____

How can you make steps toward surrendering your all to Him?

_____

_____

_____

_____

_____

_____

_____

_____

_____

_____

_____

_____

CHAPTER 6

SELF-SUFFICIENCY TO SURRENDER

I am sad to report that I have not always been as serious about surrendering to God as I am now. As I have already shared, I believed that salvation and righteousness were a result of my good works for most of my life. I remember at least one instance in which I thought, and probably said, that I do not want anyone in heaven who did not work to get there. In other words, I was putting so much effort into trying to be a righteous and saved person that I did not want anyone to have salvation that did not work at least just as hard as me for it. Glory to God for His patience, grace, mercy, and love!

According to the Bible, many people believe they are saved, but they are not. The primary reason for this crisis is because these people are trying to make it to eternity with Jesus based on their effort to do good works. Allow me to show you in the Bible. In Matthew 7:21-23, Jesus says "[21] "Not everyone who says to Me, 'Lord, Lord,' will enter the kingdom of heaven, but the one who does the will of My Father who is in heaven *will enter.* [22] Many will say to Me on that day, 'Lord, Lord, did we not prophesy in Your name, and in Your name cast out demons, and in Your name perform many [s]miracles?' [23] And then I will declare to them, 'I never knew you; leave Me, you who practice lawlessness.'"

As I have stated before, God is not looking for mere behavior modification. God wants our hearts. He wants a genuine and thriving relationship with each one of us. However, this will never happen if we depend on other than Jesus Christ for our salvation. When we try to make things happen on our own, apart from God, we are trying to be the God in our lives. There is only one foundation that is sufficient and suitable for our dependence. His name is Jesus Christ.

This point is made clear as one continues to read Matthew 7. In verses 24-27, Jesus says, "[24] "Therefore, everyone who hears these words of Mine, and [t]acts on them, will be like a wise man who built his house on the rock. [25] And the rain fell, and the [u]floods came, and the winds blew and slammed against that house; and *yet* it did not fall, for it had been founded on the rock. [26] And everyone who hears these words of Mine, and does not [v]act on them, will be like a foolish man who built his house on the sand. [27] And the rain fell, and the [w]floods came, and the winds blew and slammed against that house, and it fell—and its collapse was great."

Everyone depends on something or someone. One can choose to rely on talents, money, a spouse, etc. However, when the storms of life come, that is when we can see that God alone is worthy of our surrender and ultimate confidence. I sincerely believed for most of my life that if I went to church on the Biblical Sabbath, which is Saturday, and tried to do other things to live an honest life, that it would qualify me for salvation. I had a respect for God. However, I was mainly serving Him because I did not want to be lost. However, when I encountered the true gospel, the good news of Jesus Christ, I realized that I had it all wrong.

I have accepted Jesus as my Lord and Savior rather than myself. As a result, God has given me peace because my confidence and trust are now in Him. I have joy because He is providing for every need. My love for Him is expressed through my appreciation of Christ's sacrifice for us all. Each moment of each day, I have a passion and desire to surrender to Him. In other words, I have realized that Jesus Christ has accomplished for me what is impossible for me to achieve for myself. Therefore, instead of giving futile efforts to do His work, I accept what He has already done. If we want victory in Christ, we must first surrender to Christ.

I heard an amazing evangelist named E.E. Cleveland explain that the root of most people's difficulty to surrender to and accept salvation through Jesus is because they expect to receive good things when they work for them. If you work hard in school, you can get a good grade. If you exercise a lot, you can be in good physical health. If you are a good employee at your job, you can get a promotion. We have taught ourselves that blessings are a result of our work. Therefore, it is hard for people to comprehend God's grace. In other words, how can God save us if we did not do anything for it?

We serve a God who loves us, despite us. He looks beyond our faults, and He sees our needs. In other words, God loves us simply because we are His. Amazingly, many people need convincing before they stop working for what is already made available to them for free through Jesus. Does this mean we should not do good works? God forbid! It means, my friends, that we now have the privilege of doing good things as a demonstration and result of our love and appreciation for God. He gave His all so that we might have salvation. Thus, the appropriate response is to surrender to Him and glorify Him!

Personal Application:

Why do we try to save ourselves when only God can do it?

_____

_____

_____

_____

_____

_____

_____

_____

What do you think God will give you in exchange for

surrendering your life to Him?

_____

_____

_____

_____

_____

_____

_____

_____

_____

_____

CHAPTER 7

IT'S NOT TOO LATE

This chapter is the one chapter in this book that the devil does not want you to read. He is alright with us knowing that God is real. He may even be able to deal with us knowing that God is love. However, he does not want us to know is that there is still hope after we have messed up. In other words, the devil has done his very best to deceive multitudes into thinking that they have done too much or gone too far to be able to have a thriving soul-saving relationship with Jesus Christ. My friends, I do not have to know you personally to know that God can still meet you right where you are and redeem your life.

I have done some terrible things in my life. When I was in high school, I had an addiction to pornography, but by God's grace, He freed me from it. I am guilty of cheating, lying, stealing, bullying, and the list goes on. My sin may not be identical to your sin. In Romans 3:23, the Bible states clearly that "for all [s]have sinned and fall short of the glory of God," In other words, everyone has sinned before.

According to Romans 6:23, everyone that has sinned deserves death. We are all messed up and hopeless on our own. However, I am so glad that the verse does not end with our deserved punishment. The rest of the verse says, "…but the gracious gift of God is eternal life in Christ Jesus our Lord." This gift is available to all of us, no matter how bad we feel that we are. If you are still alive, there is still hope for you.

We see this exemplified throughout the Bible. Jesus reinstated His disciple, Peter, even after he denied Him three times. God turned Saul, a persecutor of Christians, into Paul, one of the greatest apostles of Jesus Christ that ever lived. However, perhaps the best Biblical example of God's patience and love is seen in Jesus' encounter with the thief on the cross. In Luke 23:39-43, it says, "[39] One of the criminals hanging *there* was [q]hurling abuse at Him, saying, "Are You not the [r]Christ? Save Yourself and us!" [40] But the other responded, and rebuking him, said, "Do you not even fear God, since you are under the same sentence of condemnation? [41] And we indeed *are suffering* justly, for we are receiving [s]what we deserve for our crimes, but this man has done nothing wrong." [42] And he was saying, "Jesus, remember me when You come into Your kingdom!" [43] And He said to him, "Truly, I say to you, today you will be with Me in Paradise."

Jesus was crucified with two criminals. They both deserved death for the crimes they committed. However, in the last moments of one of their lives, one of them asks for Jesus to save him. Despite all that the criminal had done wrong, Jesus chose to save the man. You have not gone too far. Don't believe the lie that you have not done too much. God loves you and still wants to save you. Even if you had already accepted Christ but turned away from Him, God can and will always save you if you let Him.

I love 2 Peter 3:9. The verse says, "The Lord is not slow about His promise, as some count slowness, but is patient toward you, not willing for any to perish, but for all to come to repentance." God is the epitome of patience. He will persistently wait and hope for us to come to our senses and choose Him. If you feel unsure that God can still make something beautiful from your life, the fact that you are even concerned about it is evidence that God is already at work in you.

It is impossible to out sin God's grace. The definition of grace is unmerited favor; it is not earned. It is just to be accepted. However, grace does not give us a license to continue in sin. Instead, accepting God's grace and mercy should be the motivation to live a life of faith and obedience to Jesus Christ. Do not listen to naysayers who say that there is no hope for you. As the saying goes, "When the devil reminds you of your past, remind him of his future." Your new start in Christ can begin right now.

If you want to surrender your life to Jesus Christ and accept Him as your Lord and Savior, pray. This simply means talk to Him. Confess that you have sinned and tell Him that you want a new start. Tell Him that you accept the sacrifice of Jesus in your place, that you accept Jesus as your Lord and Savior, and receive by faith His gift of salvation. I would recommend that you get connected to a strong Seventh-day Adventist Christian church, get more information on baptism, and enjoy your new beginning and spiritual growth in Jesus Christ. Perhaps you have been baptized, but you need to refocus on your relationship with God and want a rejuvenated connection with Him. Decide to connect with Him, and you will be making the best decision that you will ever make!

Personal Application:

How does it feel to know that there is still time for us to surrender our all to God?

_____

_____

_____

_____

_____

_____

_____

_____

_____

_____

Why is it important to submit to God as soon as possible?

_____

_____

_____

_____

_____

_____

_____

_____

_____

_____

_____

_____

CHAPTER 8

FORETOLD FRUSTRATION

I do not always feel like surrendering to God. In fact, I do not know anyone who does not want to take the easy way out from time to time and be disobedient to God. It is hard to do what is right. It is arduous, difficult, and challenging sometimes to consistently submit to God's will. This does not mean that it is a burden. It is a labor of love. However, it is still laborious. It is natural to want to give up and give in occasionally.

Throughout the entire Bible, we see examples of people who had moral failures occasioned by their frustration with the command(s) God gave them. Adam and Eve felt like God was trying to keep a good thing from them. Therefore, they ate the forbidden fruit. Moses did not want to speak to the rock for it to bring forth water. So, instead, he disobeyed God by striking the rock to get water. Even Job, one of the most righteous men that ever lived, questioned God's love and intentions towards him because of the trials that he was facing. He did not sin. Yet, it was clear that he was irritated that God was still calling him to be faithful, even after he had almost lost everything he valued in life.

The point that a lot of us miss is that God never said that following Him would be easy. In Luke 9:23-24, it says, concerning Jesus, "23 And He was saying to *them* all, "If anyone wants to come after Me, he must deny himself, take up his cross daily, and follow Me. 24 For whoever wants to save his [k]life will lose it, but whoever loses his [l]life for My sake, this is the one who will save it." To take up our cross means to sacrifice our own will, so that God's will can be done in and through our lives. It is a painful process. However, it is beyond worth it for the peace and joy that God will give us in exchange.

In 2 Timothy 3, it is made clear that all believers in Christ will face tough times. In verse 12, it says "Indeed, all who want to live in a godly way in Christ Jesus will be persecuted." It is right there, plain as day. So, is the point of this chapter to be discouraging and deter you from surrendering to God? Not at all! The point is to let you know what to expect, but still encourage you to choose Jesus anyway!

The reality is that everyone does difficult things in their lives. However, they do it because they value the prize over the price. In other words, if the reward seems worth the effort, we will do anything. For some people, this looks like sleeping outside of a store all night on Black Friday to get a good deal on an item they want. For others, this may look like studying hard in school so they can get scholarships. There are even some who will work multiple jobs so they can provide for their family. Everyone has at least one thing in their life that they would do anything for. The simple admonition of this chapter is to make Jesus that highest priority in our lives.

I love God with everything within me. However, I still find it difficult to surrender to Him sometimes because I know He may impress me to do something that I do not feel like doing. Yet, when I think of the goodness of Jesus, and all that He has done for me, I cannot help but obey Him. He is what is most important in my heart. Therefore, I will do whatever it takes to make Him happy. Whether you love God or not, I hope that you realize that He already loves you. Whether you choose God or not, I hope that you realize that He has already chosen you.

When we surrender to God, it leads to a blessed and abundant life. When we do not, it leads to despair, depression, and degradation. If you go back to Luke 9, you will see in verse 25 that the question is asked "For what good does it do a person if he gains the whole world, but loses or forfeits himself?" My friends, is that sin worth losing your eternal salvation? God is giving you a chance to make the right choice. Jesus gave His life, so that we may have life. In return, you do not have to be flawless. Yet, by the power of The Holy Spirit, may we all seek to be faithful to Christ.

Personal Application:

How liberating is it to know that frustration with God is not a sin?

_____

_____

_____

_____

_____

_____

_____

_____

_____

Are there any feelings of frustration that you need to share with God? What would it look like if you shared those with Him today?

_____

_____

_____

_____

_____

_____

_____

_____

_____

CHAPTER 9

THE MIND FACTOR

The brain is the control center of the body. Therefore, if something or someone has our mind, then our whole being is captured. Hence, God and Satan are in conflict over our minds. Through media, church, school, etc., we are continually being bombarded by messages. Some of it is true. The rest is false. Thankfully, we have free will and the ability to invest in our minds' health by nurturing it with things that will help us focus on, and ultimately surrender to, Jesus Christ.

There are numerous times that the Bible mentions the importance of having clear thoughts because, without clearness of mind, we are more likely to succumb to the schemes of the devil. The following are some examples. 1 Peter 1:13 says, "Therefore, [i]prepare your minds for action, [i]keep sober *in spirit*, set your hope completely on the grace to be brought to you at the revelation of Jesus Christ." 1 Peter 5:8 says, "Be of sober *spirit*, be on the alert. Your adversary, the devil, prowls around like a roaring lion, seeking someone to devour." Finally, Romans 12:1-2 says, "Therefore I urge you, brothers *and sisters*, by the mercies of God, to present your bodies as a living and holy sacrifice, [a]acceptable to God, *which is* your [b]spiritual service of worship. [2] And do not be conformed to this [c]world, but be transformed by the renewing of your mind, so that you may [d]prove what the will of God is, that which is good and [e]acceptable and perfect."

Mental health plays a critical role in spirituality. God only wants us to engage in things that will help us think clearer because, if we do not, it is easier for us to be deceived by the devil. So, how can we have optimal mental health? Obtaining optimal mental health can be done in a variety of ways. When we eat healthy brain-boosting food, such as fruits and vegetables, it improves and elevates our thinking level. In Daniel 1, Daniel and his friends chose to eat only vegetables and water for ten days, and then they compared to the other youth who ate the king's food. At the end of the ten days, Daniel and his friends were better in their thinking, appearance, and every other way, because of God blessing them through their diet.

Some people believe that what they behold does not affect them. However, this idea could not be more wrong. In 2 Corinthians 3:18, the Bible says, "But we all, with unveiled faces, looking as in a mirror at the glory of the Lord, are being transformed into the same image from glory to glory, just as from the Lord, the Spirit." In other words, what we see and listen to has an impact on us. It changes who we are. Therefore, another key to optimal brain function is to behold things that are positive and glorify God. I am not saying that everything you watch or listen to has to be overtly Christian. However, we should only take in things that promote the ideals we find in the Bible.

In my opinion, the best brain-boosting music is Christian classical music. However, I also listen to gospel, Christian contemporary, and other music genres that help me live a joyous and surrendered life to Christ. As far as the things I watch on T.V., I like to watch channels such as 3ABN and Hope Channel, sports, and other family-friendly content. My viewing selection is not perfect. However, I try to be intentional about only taking in things that do not lead to negative actions. Also, never underestimate the importance of regularly reading the Bible. It can improve brain function better than any other book.

The main principles of health are summarized in an acronym named N.E.W. S.T.A.R.T. I did not create this acronym. However, I find it very helpful. It stands for nutrition, exercise, water, sunlight, temperance, air, rest, and trust in God. If we do these things, our thinking will be better, also our overall health. Another excellent resource for optimal brain function is a book entitled "The Lost Art of Thinking" by Dr. Neil Nedley. Through this book and other resources, he has given great and practical tips, backed up by sound research, to think better and live better.

What is on your mind? The answer to this question is more important than many people realize. This chapter is just a summary of some things that can help us think better. Many would be surprised by the clarity of mind they could experience by utilizing this information. Of course, there are more specific things that can be done to think more clearly. However, I hope that this summary gives you a great starting point. The devil wants to confuse and deceive us. God wants us to think as clearly as possible so we can see that He alone is worthy of our surrender.

Personal Application:

What are some things that you can do today to think more clearly?

_____

_____

_____

_____

_____

_____

_____

_____

How does understanding that God wants us to think critically influence your view of Him?

_____

_____

_____

_____

_____

_____

_____

_____

_____

CHAPTER 10

THE PATHWAY TO PEACE

There comes a point in every person's life where we must decide who we will serve. I believe this book has provided enough information to make an educated decision on the matter. Enough is enough. Will we choose life or death? In other words, will we choose Jesus or the devil? No one can decide for you. However, only one option is worth it. Also, I can personally tell you that Jesus is the best thing that has ever happened to me.

Typically, when people talk about surrender, they depict it negatively. To surrender means to give up or give in. Most people view submitting fully to God as losing. The reality is that, in most cases, surrendering does mean to lose. However, when one surrenders to God, it does not lead to defeat. It leads to victory. When we surrender to God, we give up our right to call the shots in our lives. If we submit to God, we are allowing Him to have His way in our lives. Allowing Him to have His way leads to blessings for us and others, and ultimately it leads to God's glory.

John 3:16 says "[16] "For God so loved the world, that He gave His [c]only begotten Son, that whoever believes in Him shall not perish, but have eternal life." This verse is probably the most popular text in the Bible. However, unfortunately, it is also perhaps the most misunderstood. The verse makes clear what God wants everyone to have. It is salvation. However, just because He wants you to have it does not necessarily mean you do. In other words, the freedom of salvation is a gift for you. It is not yours until you choose to accept it.

But before you do, I need to let you know that God inspired me to write this book to warn you that choosing Jesus comes at a cost. As it says in Matthew 6:24, "No one can serve two masters…" The Bible tells us that God is a jealous God. He does not want just some of you. Just having most of you is not an option for Him. He wants it all! Having all of us cannot happen while we are still holding on to sin.

I have heard that men who catch animals in Africa for American zoos say that one of the most challenging animals to capture is the ring-tailed monkey. But the Zulus from Africa have found a simple way to do it. In fact, they have been catching these nimble little animals for years. The way that they do it is that they use their knowledge of the animal to capture it. They do not use an elaborate and meticulous contraption. They do not need to utilize weapons and heavy artillery. Their trap is nothing more than a melon that is growing from a vine.

The Zulus know that this melon's seeds are a favorite of the monkey. So, the Zulus cut a hole in the melon, just large enough for the monkey to put in his hand to reach the seeds in it. The monkey will insert his hand, grab as many seeds as possible, and then remove them. However, he cannot because his fist is now bigger than the hole. The monkey will yank and pull, scream, and fight the melon for hours. But the monkey can't get free of the trap because he refuses to let go of the thing that keeps him in bondage! As the monkey struggles, the Zulus sneak up and capture it.

My friends, the key to true freedom in this life is to let go of the things that bind us. Jesus is always knocking at the doors of our hearts. He is petitioning us to choose Him so that He can give us abundant and eternal life. Choosing Jesus is the only way we win from surrendering. He loves us more than words can describe. If you now realize the importance of having an ever-growing and soul-saving relationship with Jesus Christ, I implore you to give Him a chance. When we surrender our lives to Him, it does not mean that we will never face hardships again. However, we can have peace, joy, and hope as He carries us through them. Please do not wait another second. Jesus is the key to your breakthrough! By the power of The Holy Spirit, may we surrender our all to The One who generously gave His all so that we could be free.

Personal Application:

How has this book impacted your life?

_____

_____

_____

_____

_____

_____

_____

_____

_____

Will you fully surrender to God? Surrendering does not mean that you will be perfect. However, by God's grace, the goal is to be faithful.

_____

_____

_____

_____

_____

_____

_____

_____

_____

_____

ABOUT THE AUTHOR

Minister Michael Boddie II loves God with everything within him. He was born and raised as a Seventh-day Adventist Christian; and God has always played a huge role in his life. Minister Boddie has a Bachelor of Arts degree in Ministerial Theology from Oakwood University and has served in several roles in ministry, including being a lay-pastor and Bible worker. Currently, he is pursuing a Master of Divinity degree and is a chaplain resident with Kettering Health Network in the Dayton, Ohio area. More than anything else, Minister Boddie wants the world to know that Jesus saves, and we can always find hope through Him.

Made in the USA
Monee, IL
28 October 2024

68851609R00031